SIX RESIDUA

From the same publishers

Samuel Beckett

Novels

Dream of Fair to Middling Women (1932)
Murphy (1938)
Watt (1945)
First Love (1945)
Mercier and Camier (1946)
Molloy (1951)*
Malone Dies (1951)*

The Unnamable (1953) *
How It Is (1961)
Company (1980)**
Ill Seen Ill Said (1981)**
Worstward Ho (1983)**

* published together as the Trilogy

** published together as Nohow On

Short Prose

More Pricks than Kicks (1934)
Collected Short Prose (in preparation)
Beckett Shorts (see below)

Poetry

Collected Poems (1930-1978)
Anthology of Mexican Poetry
(translations)

Criticism

Proust & Three Dialogues with Georges Duthuit (1931,1949)
Disjecta (1929-1967)

Beckett Shorts (A collection of 12 short volumes to commemorate the writer's death in 1989)

1. Texts for Nothing (1947-52)
2. Dramatic Works and Dialogues (1938-67)
3. All Strange Away (1963)
4. Worstward Ho (1983)
5. Six Residua (1957-72)
6. For to End Yet Again (1960-75)

7. The Old Tune (1962)
8. First Love (1945)
9. As the Story Was Told
10. Three Novellas (1945-6)
11. Stirrings Still (1986-9)
12. Selected Poems (1930-85)

SIX RESIDUA

Samuel Beckett

John Calder
London

This volume first published 1999 as a collection in Great Britain by John
Calder Publishers
London

Six Residua First published in Great Britain in 1978 by John Calder Ltd.
From an Abandoned Work first published by Faber & Faber London,
1958. Reprinted by Calder & Boyars in *No's Knife* 1967,1975
Enough originally published by Les Editions de Minuit, Paris, as *Assez*,
1966. First published in Great Britain in *No's Knife* by Calder & Boyars,
1967,1975
Imagination Dead Imagine originally published by Les Editions De
Minuit, Paris, as *Imagination Morte Imaginez*, 1965 and by Calder &
Boyars, London 1966. Reprinted by Calder & Boyars 1967,1975
Ping originally published by Les Editions De Minuit, Paris, as *Bing*,
1966. First published in Great Britain in *No's Knife* by Calder & Boyars,
1967,1975
Lessness originally published by Les Editions De Minuit, Paris, as *Sans,*
1969. First published in Great Britain by Calder & Boyars, 1970
The Lost Ones originally published by Les Editions Minuit, Paris as *Le
Depeupleur,* 1971. First published in Great Britain by Calder & Boyars,
1972
© Les Editions De Minuit

© All material in this volume Samuel Beckett Estate 1999
ISBN 0 7145 36636 Paperback

British Library Cataloguing in Publication Data
A catalogue record for this title is available from the British Library

Printed by Webcom, Canada

CONTENTS

PREFACE

This volume contains six texts by Samuel Beckett which were first published between 1957 and 1972. All of them are residues of longer works which were either abandoned or condensed. In spite of their brevity they have been singled out by critics and scholars as work of the first quality and significance and among the most important in the Beckett canon.

From an Abandoned Work, as its title implies, is an unfinished fragment, first published by Faber and Faber in 1958, having been previously broadcast by the BBC in 1957 with the voice of Patrick Magee, produced by Donald McWhinnie. It was collected in 1967 in *No's Knife*, a volume containing the author's short prose from 1945 to 1966.

Imagination Dead Imagine, *Enough* and *Ping* were also last published in *No's Knife*, although the first of these residua had separate publication in February 1966. All three are translated from the original French and came from the same collection of prose in manuscript that was originally intended to be a single long work. *Enough* first appeared as *Assez* in the first edition of *La Quinzaine Litteraire* in 1966 and was later published, like all of Mr Beckett's work, by *Les Editions de Minuit*. *Ping* was entitled *Bing* in French and published in Paris in 1966 and London in 1967.

Lessness was published in France under the title *Sans* in 1969 and a year later in Britain. Coming as it did shortly after Samuel Beckett received the Nobel Prize, it received a quite exceptional British press. It was broadcast by the BBC in February 1971, produced by Martin Esslin with the voices of Harold Pinter, Nicol Williamson, Patrick Magee, Donal Donally, Leonard Fenton and Denys Hawthorne, each representing one of the tribes involved in the narrative.

The Lost Ones first appeared as *Le Depeupleur* in 1971 and in translation in 1972. The current volume is its third printing. All texts with the exception of *From an Abandoned Work* were written by Mr Beckett first in French and subsequently translated by him.

The Publishers

FROM AN ABANDONED WORK

FROM AN ABANDONED WORK

Up bright and early that day, I was young then, feeling awful, and out, mother hanging out of the window in her nightdress weeping and waving. Nice fresh morning, bright too early as so often. Feeling really awful, very violent. The sky would soon darken and rain fall and go on falling, all day, till evening. Then blue and sun again a second, then night. Feeling all this, how violent and the kind of day, I stopped and turned. So back with bowed head on the look out for a snail, slug or worm. Great love in my heart too for all things still and rooted, bushes, boulders and the like, too numerous to mention, even the flowers of the field, not for the world when in my right senses would I ever touch one, to pluck it. Whereas a bird now, or a butterfly, fluttering about and getting in my way, all moving things, getting in my path, a slug now, getting under my feet, no, no mercy. Not that I'd go out of my way to get at them, no, at a distance often they seemed still, then a moment later they were upon me. Birds with my piercing sight I have seen flying so high, so far, that they seemed at rest, then the next minute they were all about me, crows have done this. Ducks are perhaps the worst, to be suddenly stamping and stumbling in the midst of ducks, or hens, any class of poultry, few things are worse. Nor will I go out of my way to avoid such things, when avoidable, no, I simply will not go out of my way, though I have never in my life been on my way anywhere, but simply on my way. And in this way I have gone through great thickets, bleeding, and deep into bogs, water too, even the sea in some moods and been carried out of my course, or driven back, so as not to drown. And that is perhaps how I shall die at last if they don't catch me, I mean drowned, or in fire, yes, perhaps that is how I shall do it at last, walking furious headlong into fire and dying burnt to bits. Then I raised my eyes and saw my mother still in the window waving, waving me back or on I don't know, or just waving, in sad helpless love, and I heard faintly her cries. The window-frame was green, pale, the house-wall grey and my mother white and so thin I could see past her (piercing sight I had then) into the dark of the room, and on all that full the not long risen sun, and all small because of the distance, very pretty really the whole thing, I remember it, the old grey and then the thin green surround and the thin white against the dark, if only she could have been still and let me look at it all. No, for once I wanted to stand and look at something I couldn't with her there waving and fluttering and swaying in and out of the window as though she were doing exercises, and for all I know she may have been, not bothering about me at all. No tenacity of purpose, that was another thing I didn't like in her. One week it would be exercises, and the next prayers and Bible reading, and the next gardening, and the next playing the piano and singing, that was awful, and then just lying about and resting, always changing. Not that it mattered to me, I was always out. But let me get on now with the day I have hit on to begin with, any other would have done as well, yes, on with it and out of my way and on to another, enough of my mother for the moment. Well then for a time all well, no trouble, no birds at me, nothing across my path except at a great distance a white horse followed by a boy, or it might have been a small man or woman. This is the only completely white horse I remember, what I believe the Germans call a Schimmel, oh I was very quick as a boy and picked up a lot of hard knowledge, Schimmel, nice word, for an English speaker. The sun was full upon it, as shortly before on my mother, and it seemed to have a red band or stripe running down its side, I thought perhaps a bellyband, perhaps the horse was going somewhere to be harnessed, to a trap or suchlike. It crossed my path a long way off, then vanished behind greenery, I suppose, all I noticed was the sudden appearance of the horse, then disappearance. It was bright white, with the sun on it, I had never seen such a horse, though often heard of them, and never saw another. White I must say has always affected me strongly, all white things, sheets, walls and so on, even flowers, and then just white, the thought of white, without more. But let me get on with this day and get it over. All well then for a time, just the violence and then this white horse, when suddenly I flew into a most savage rage, really blinding. Now why this sudden rage I really don't know, these sudden rages, they made my life a misery. Many other things too did this, my sore throat for example, I have never known what it is to be without a sore throat, but the rages were the worst, like a great wind suddenly rising in me, no, I can't describe. It wasn't the violence getting worse in any case, nothing to do with that, some days I would be feeling violent all day and never have a rage, other days quite quiet for me and have four or five. No, there's no accounting for it, there's no accounting for anything, with a mind like the one I always had, always on the alert against itself, I'll come back on this perhaps when I feel less weak. There was a time I tried to get relief by beating my head against some-

thing, but I gave it up. The best thing I found was to
start running. Perhaps I should mention here I was a
very slow walker. I didn't dally or loiter in any way,
just walked very slowly, little short steps and the feet
very slow through the air. On the other hand I must
have been quite one of the fastest runners the world
has ever seen, over a short distance, five or ten yards,
in a second I was there. But I could not go on at that
speed, not for breathlessness, it was mental, all is
mental, figments. Now the jog trot on the other hand,
I could no more do that than I could fly. No, with me
all was slow, and then these flashes, or gushes, vent the
pent, that was one of those things I used to say, over
and over, as I went along, vent the pent, vent the
pent. Fortunately my father died when I was a boy,
otherwise I might have been a professor, he had set
his heart on it. A very fair scholar I was too, no thought,
but a great memory. One day I told him about
Milton's cosmology, away up in the mountains we
were, resting against a huge rock looking out to sea,
that impressed him greatly. Love too, often in my
thoughts, when a boy, but not a great deal compared
to other boys, it kept me awake I found. Never loved
anyone I think, I'd remember. Except in my dreams,
and there it was animals, dream animals, nothing like
what you see walking about the country, I couldn't
describe them, lovely creatures they were, white
mostly. In a way perhaps it's a pity, a good woman
might have been the making of me, I might be sprawl-
ing in the sun now sucking my pipe and patting the
bottoms of the third and fourth generation, looked up
to and respected, wondering what there was for dinner,
instead of stravaging the same old roads in all weathers,
I was never much of a one for new ground. No, I regret nothing, all I regret is having been born, dying is

such a long tiresome business I always found. But let me get on now from where I left off, the white horse and then the rage, no connexion I suppose. But why go on with all this, I don't know, some day I must end, why not now. But these are thoughts, not mine, no matter, shame upon me. Now I am old and weak, in pain and weakness murmur why and pause, and the old thoughts well up in me and over into my voice, the old thoughts born with me and grown with me and kept under, there's another. No, back to that far day, any far day, and from the dim granted ground to its things and sky the eyes raised and back again, raised again and back again again, and the feet going nowhere only somehow home, in the morning out from home and in the evening back home again, and the sound of my voice all day long muttering the same old things I don't listen to, not even mine it was at the end of the day, like a marmoset sitting on my shoulder with its bushy tail, keeping me company. All this talking, very low and hoarse, no wonder I had a sore throat. Perhaps I should mention here that I never talked to anyone, I think my father was the last one I talked to. My mother was the same, never talked, never answered, since my father died. I asked her for the money, I can't go back on that now, those must have been my last words to her. Sometimes she cried out on me, or implored, but never long, just a few cries, then if I looked up the poor old thin lips pressed tight together and the body turned away and just the corners of the eyes on me, but it was rare. Sometimes in the night I heard her, talking to herself I suppose, or praying out loud, or reading out loud, or reciting her hymns, poor woman. Well after the horse and rage I don't know, just on, then I suppose the slow turn, wheeling more and more to the one or other hand, till facing home, then home. Ah my father and mother, to think they are probably in paradise, they were so good. Let me go to hell, that's all I ask, and go on cursing them there, and them look down and hear me, that might take some of the shine off their bliss. Yes, I believe all their blather about the life to come, it cheers me up, and unhappiness like mine, there's no annihilating that. I was mad of course and still am, but harmless, I passed for harmless, that's a good one. Not of course that I was really mad, just strange, a little strange, and with every passing year a little stranger, there can be few stranger creatures going about than me at the present day. My father, did I kill him too as well as my mother, perhaps in a way I did, but I can't go into that now, much too old and weak. The questions float up as I go along and leave me very confused, breaking up I am. Suddenly they are there, no, they float up, out of an old depth, and hover and linger before they die away, questions that when I was in my right mind would not have survived one second, no, but atomized they would have been, before as much as formed, atomized. In twos often they came, one hard on the other, thus, How shall I go on another day? and then, How did I ever go on another day? Or, Did I kill my father? and then, Did I ever kill anyone? That kind of way, to the general from the particular I suppose you might say, question and answer too in a way, very addling. I strive with them as best I can, quickening my step when they come on, tossing my head from side to side and up and down, staring agonizedly at this and that, increasing my murmur to a scream, these are helps. But they should not be necessary, something is wrong here, if it was the end I would not so much mind, but how often I have said, in my life, before some new awful thing, It is the end, and it was not the end, and yet the end cannot be far off now, I shall fall as I go along and stay down or curl up for the night as usual among the rocks and before morning be gone. Oh I know I too shall cease and be as when I was not yet, only all over instead of in store, that makes me happy, often now my murmur falters and dies and I weep for happiness as I go along and for love of this old earth that has carried me so long and whose uncomplainingness will soon be mine. Just under the surface I shall be, all together at first, then separate and drift, through all the earth and perhaps in the end through a cliff into the sea, something of me. A ton of worms in an acre, that is a wonderful thought, a ton of worms, I believe it. Where did I get it, from a dream, or a book read in a nook when a boy, or a word overheard as I went along, or in me all along and kept under till it could give me joy, these are the kind of horrid thoughts I have to contend with in the way I have said. Now is there nothing to add to this day with the white horse and white mother in the window, please read again my descriptions of these, before I get on to some other day at a later time, nothing to add before I move on in time skipping hundreds and even thousands of days in a way I could not at the time, but had to get through somehow until I came to the one I am coming to now, no, nothing, all has gone but mother in the window, the violence, rage and rain. So on to this second day and get it over and out of the way and on to the next. What happens now is I was set on and pursued by a family or tribe, I do not know, of stoats, a most extraordinary thing, I think they were stoats. Indeed if I may say so I think I was fortunate to get off with my life, strange expression, it does not sound right somehow. Anyone else would have been bitten and bled to death, perhaps sucked white, like a rabbit, there is that word white again. I

know I could never think, but if I could have, and then
had, I would just have lain down and let myself be
destroyed, as the rabbit does. But let me start as always
with the morning and the getting out. When a day
comes back, whatever the reason, then its morning and
its evening too are there, though in themselves quite
unremarkable, the going out and coming home, there
is a remarkable thing I find. So up then in the grey of
dawn, very weak and shaky after an atrocious night
little dreaming what lay in store, out and off. What time
of year, I really do not know, does it matter. Not wet
really, but dripping, everything dripping, the day
might rise, did it, no, drip drip all day long, no sun, no
change of light, dim all day, and still, not a breath, till
night, then black, and a little wind, I saw some stars,
as I neared home. My stick of course, by a merciful
providence, I shall not say this again, when not
mentioned my stick is in my hand, as I go along. But
not my long coat, just my jacket, I could never bear
the long coat, flapping about my legs, or rather one
day suddenly I turned against it, a sudden violent dis-
like. Often when dressed to go I would take it out and
put it on, then stand in the middle of the room unable
to move, until at last I could take it off and put it back
on its hanger, in the cupboard. But I was hardly down
the stairs and out into the air when the stick fell from
my hand and I just sank to my knees to the ground and
then forward on my face, a most extraordinary thing,
and then after a little over on my back, I could never
lie on my face for any length of time, much as I loved
it, it made me feel sick, and lay there, half an hour
perhaps, with my arms along my sides and the palms
of my hands against the pebbles and my eyes wide
open straying over the sky. Now was this my first experience of this kind, that is the question that im-

mediately assails one. Falls I had had in plenty, of the kind after which unless a limb broken you pick yourself up and go on, cursing God and man, very different from this. With so much life gone from knowledge how know when all began, all the variants of the one that one by one their venom staling follow upon one another, all life long, till you succumb. So in some way even olden things each time are first things, no two breaths the same, all a going over and over and all once and never more. But let me get up now and on and get this awful day over and on to the next. But what is the sense of going on with all this, there is none. Day after unremembered day until my mother's death, then in a new place soon old until my own. And when I come to this night here among the rocks with my two books and the strong starlight it will have passed from me and the day that went before, my two books, the little and the big, all past and gone, or perhaps just moments here and there still, this little sound perhaps now that I don't understand so that I gather up my things and go back into my hole, so bygone they can be told. Over, over, there is a soft place in my heart for all that is over, no, for the being over, I love the word, words have been my only loves, not many. Often all day long as I went along I have said it, and sometimes I would be saying vero, oh vero. Oh but for those awful fidgets I have always had I would have lived my life in a big empty echoing room with a big old pendulum clock, just listening and dozing, the case open so that I could watch the swinging, moving my eyes to and fro, and the lead weights dangling lower and lower till I got up out of my chair and wound them up again, once a week. The third day was the look I got from the roadman, suddenly I see that now, the ragged old brute bent double down in the ditch leaning on his spade or whatever it was and leering round and up at me from under the brim of his slouch, the red mouth, how is it I wonder I saw him at all, that is more like it, the day I saw the look I got from Balfe, I went in terror of him as a child. Now he is dead and I resemble him. But let us get on and leave these old scenes and come to these, and my reward. Then it will not be as now, day after day, out, on, round, back, in, like leaves turning, or torn out and thrown crumpled away, but a long unbroken time without before or after, light or dark, from or towards or at, the old half knowledge of when and where gone, and of what, but kinds of things still, all at once, all going, until nothing, there was never anything, never can be, life and death all nothing, that kind of thing, only a voice dreaming and droning on all around, that is something, the voice that once was in your mouth. Well once out on the road and free of the property what then, I really do not know, the next thing I was up in the bracken lashing about with my stick making the drops fly and cursing, filthy language, the same words over and over, I hope nobody heard me. Throat very bad, to swallow was torment, and something wrong with an ear, I kept poking at it without relief, old wax perhaps pressing on the drum. Extraordinary still over the land, and in me too all quite still, a coincidence, why the curses were pouring out of me I do not know, no, that is a foolish thing to say, and the lashing about with the stick, what possessed me mild and weak to be doing that, as I struggled along. Is it the stoats now, no, first I just sink down again and disappear in the ferns, up to my waist they were as I went along. Harsh things these great ferns, like starched, very woody, terrible stalks, take the skin off your legs through your trousers, and then the holes they hide, break your leg if you're not careful, awful English this, fall and vanish from view, you could lie there for weeks and no one hear you, I often thought of that up in the mountains, no, that is a foolish thing to say, just went on, my body doing its best without me.

ENOUGH

ENOUGH

All that goes before forget. Too much at a time is too much. That gives the pen time to note. I don't see it but I hear it there behind me. Such is the silence. When the pen stops I go on. Sometimes it refuses. When it refuses I go on. Too much silence is too much. Or it's my voice too weak at times. The one that comes out of me. So much for the art and craft.

I did all he desired. I desired it too. For him. Whenever he desired something so did I. He only had to say what thing. When he didn't desire anything neither did I. In this way I didn't live without desires. If he had desired something for me I would have desired it too. Happiness for example or fame. I only had the desires he manifested. But he must have manifested them all. All his desires and needs. When he was silent he must have been like me. When he told me to lick his penis I hastened to do so. I drew satisfaction from it. We must have had the same satisfactions. The same needs and the same satisfactions.

One day he told me to leave him. It's the verb he used. He must have been on his last legs. I don't know if by that he meant me to leave him for good or only to step aside a moment. I never asked myself the question. I never asked myself any questions but his. Whatever it was he meant I made off without looking back. Gone from reach of his voice I was gone from his life. Perhaps it was that he desired. There are questions you see and don't ask yourself. He must have been on his last legs. I on the contrary was far from on my last legs. I belonged to an entirely different generation. It didn't last. Now that I'm entering night I have kinds of gleams in my skull. Stony ground but not entirely. Given three or four lives I might have accomplished something.

I cannot have been more than six when he took me by the hand. Barely emerging from childhood. But it didn't take me long to emerge altogether. It was the left hand. To be on the right was more than he could bear. We advanced side by side hand in hand. One pair of gloves was enough. The free or outer hands hung bare. He did not like to feel against his skin the skin of another. Mucous membrane is a different matter. Yet he sometimes took off his glove. Then I had to take off mine. We would cover in this way a hundred yards or so linked by our bare extremities. Seldom more. That was enough for him. If the question were put to me I would say that odd hands are ill-fitted for intimacy. Mine never felt at home in his. Sometimes they let each other go. The clasp loosened and they fell apart. Whole minutes often passed before they clasped again. Before his clasped mine again.

They were cotton gloves rather tight. Far from blunting the shapes they sharpened them by simplifying. Mine was naturally too loose for years. But it didn't take me long to fill it. He said I had Aquarius hands. It's a mansion above.

All I know comes from him. I won't repeat this apropos of all my bits of knowledge. The art of combining is not my fault. It's a curse from above. For the rest I would suggest not guilty.

Our meeting. Though very bowed already he looked a giant to me. In the end his trunk ran parallel with the ground. To counterbalance this anomaly he held his legs apart and sagged at the knees. His feet grew more and more flat and splay. His horizon was the ground they trod. Tiny moving carpet of turf and trampled flowers. He gave me his hand like a tired old ape with the elbow lifted as high as it would go. I had only to straighten up to be head and shoulders above him. One day he halted and fumbling for his words explained to me that anatomy is a whole.

In the beginning he always spoke walking. So it seems to me now. Then sometimes walking and sometimes still. In the end still only. And the voice getting fainter all the time. To save him having to say the same thing twice running I bowed right down. He halted and waited for me to get into position. As soon as out of the corner of his eye he glimpsed my head alongside his the murmurs came. Nine times out of ten they did not concern me. But he wished everything to be heard including the ejaculations and broken paternosters that he poured out to the flowers at his feet.

He halted then and waited for my head to arrive before telling me to leave him. I snatched away my hand and made off without looking back. Two steps and I was lost to him for ever. We were severed if that is what he desired.

His talk was seldom of geodesy. But we must have covered several times the equivalent of the terrestrial equator. At an average speed of roughly three miles per day and night. We took flight in arithmetic. What mental calculations bent double hand in hand! Whole ternary numbers we raised in this way to the third power sometimes in downpours of rain. Graving themselves in his memory as best they could the ensuing cubes accumulated. In view of the converse operation at a later stage. When time would have done its work.

If the question were put to me suitably framed I would say yes indeed the end of this long outing was my life. Say about the last seven thousand miles. Counting from the day when alluding for the first time to his infirmity he said he thought it had reached its peak. The future proved him right. That part of it at least we were to make past of together.

I see the flowers at my feet and it's the others I see. Those we trod down with equal step. It is true they are the same.

Contrary to what I had long been pleased to imagine he was not blind. Merely indolent. One day he halted and fumbling for his words described his vision. He concluded by saying he thought it would get no worse. How far this was not a delusion I cannot say. I never asked myself the question. When I bowed down to receive his communications I felt on my eye a glint of blue bloodshot apparently affected.

He sometimes halted without saying anything. Either he had finally nothing to say or while having something to say he finally decided not to say it. I bowed down as usual to save him having to repeat himself and we remained in this position. Bent double heads touching silent hand in hand. While all about us fast on one another the minutes flew. Sooner or later his foot broke away from the flowers and we moved on. Perhaps only to halt again after a few steps. So that he might say at last what was in his heart or decide not to say it again.

Other main examples suggest themselves to the mind. Immediate continuous communication with immediate redeparture. Same thing with delayed redeparture. Delayed continuous communication with immediate redeparture. Same thing with delayed redeparture. Immediate discontinuous communication with immediate redeparture. Same thing with delayed redeparture. Delayed discontinuous communication with immediate redeparture. Same thing with delayed redeparture.

It is then I shall have lived then or never. Ten years at the very least. From the day he drew the back of his left hand lingeringly over his sacral ruins and launched his prognostic. To the day of my supposed disgrace. I can see the place a step short of the crest. Two steps forward and I was descending the other slope. If I had looked back I would not have seen him.

He loved to climb and therefore I too. He clamoured for the steepest slopes. His human frame broke down into two equal segments. This thanks to the shortening of the lower by the sagging knees. On a gradient of one in one his head swept the ground. To what this taste was due I cannot say. To love of the earth and the flowers' thousand scents and hues. Or to cruder imperatives of an anatomical order. He never raised the question. The crest once reached alas the going down again.

In order from time to time to enjoy the sky he resorted to a little round mirror. Having misted it with his breath and polished it on his calf he looked in it for the constellations. I have it! he exclaimed referring to the Lyre or the Swan. And often he added that the sky seemed much the same.

We were not in the mountains however. There were times I discerned on the horizon a sea whose level seemed higher than ours. Could it be the bed of some vast evaporated lake or drained of its waters from below? I never asked myself the question.

The fact remains we often came upon this sort of mound some three hundred feet in height. Reluctantly I raised my eyes and discerned the nearest often on the horizon. Or instead of moving on from the one we had just descended we ascended it again.

I am speaking of our last decade comprised between the two events described. It veils those that went before and must have resembled it like blades of grass. To those engulfed years it is reasonable to impute my education. For I don't remember having learnt anything in those I remember. It is with this reasoning I calm myself when brought up short by all I know.

I set the scene of my disgrace just short of a crest. On the contrary it was on the flat in a great calm. If I had looked back I would have seen him in the place where I had left him. Some trifle would have shown me my mistake if mistake there had been. In the years that followed I did not exclude the possibility of finding him again. In the place where I had left him if not elsewhere. Or of hearing him call me. At the same time telling myself he was on his last legs. But I did not count on it unduly. For I hardly raised my eyes from the flowers. And his voice was spent. And as if that were not enough I kept telling myself he was on his last legs. So it did not take me long to stop counting on it altogether.

I don't know what the weather is now. But in my life it was eternally mild. As if the earth had come to rest in spring. I am thinking of our hemisphere. Sudden pelting downpours overtook us. Without noticeable darkening of the sky. I would not have noticed the windlessness if he had not spoken of it. Of the wind that was no more. Of the storms he had ridden out. It is only fair to say there was nothing to sweep away. The very flowers were stemless and flush with the ground like water-lilies. No brightening our buttonholes with these.

We did not keep tally of the days. If I arrive at ten years it is thanks to our podometer. Total milage divided by average daily milage. So many days. Divide. Such a figure the night before the sacrum. Such another the eve of my disgrace. Daily average always up to date. Subtract. Divide.

Night. As long as day in this endless equinox. It falls and we go on. Before dawn we are gone.

Attitude at rest. Wedged together bent in three. Second right angle at the knees. I on the inside. We turn over as one man when he manifests the desire. I can feel him at night pressed against me with all his twisted length. It was less a matter of sleeping than of lying down. For we walked in a half sleep. With his upper hand he held and touched me where he wished. Up to a certain point. The other was twined in my hair. He murmured of things that for him were no more and for me could not have been. The wind in the overground stems. The shade and shelter of the forests.

He was not given to talk. An average of a hundred words per day and night. Spaced out. A bare million in all. Numerous repeats. Ejaculations. Too few for even a cursory survey. What do I know of man's destiny? I could tell you more about radishes. For them he had a fondness. If I saw one I would name it without hesitation.

We lived on flowers. So much for sustenance. He halted and without having to stoop caught up a handful of petals. Then moved munching on. They had on the whole a calming action. We were on the whole calm. More and more. All was. This notion of calm comes from him. Without him I would not have had it. Now I'll wipe out everything but the flowers. No more rain. No more mounds. Nothing but the two of us dragging through the flowers. Enough my old breasts feel his old hand.

Translated from the French by the author

IMAGINATION DEAD IMAGINE

IMAGINATION DEAD IMAGINE

No trace anywhere of life, you say, pah, no difficulty there, imagination not dead yet, yes, dead, good, imagination dead imagine. Islands, waters, azure, verdure, one glimpse and vanished, endlessly, omit. Till all white in the whiteness the rotunda. No way in, go in, measure. Diameter three feet, three feet from ground to summit of the vault. Two diameters at right angles AB CD divide the white ground into two semicircles ACB BDA. Lying on the ground two white bodies, each in its semicircle. White too the vault and the round wall eighteen inches high from which it springs. Go back out, a plain rotunda, all white in the whiteness, go back in, rap, solid throughout, a ring as in the imagination the ring of bone. The light that makes all so white no visible source, all shines with the same white shine, ground, wall, vault, bodies, no shadow. Strong heat, surfaces hot but not burning to the touch, bodies sweating. Go back out, move back, the little fabric vanishes, ascend, it vanishes, all white in the whiteness, descend, go back in. Emptiness, silence, heat, whiteness, wait, the light goes down, all grows dark together, ground, wall, vault, bodies, say twenty seconds, all the greys, the light goes out, all vanishes. At the same time the temperature goes down, to reach its minimum, say freezing-point, at the same instant that the black is reached, which may seem strange. Wait, more or less long, light and heat come back, all grows white and hot together, ground, wall, vault, bodies, say twenty seconds, all the greys, till the initial level is reached whence the fall began. More or less long, for there may intervene, experience shows, between end of fall and beginning of rise, pauses of varying length, from the fraction of the second to what would have seemed, in other times, other places, an eternity. Same remark for the other pause, between end of rise and beginning of fall. The extremes, as long as they last, are perfectly stable, which in the case of the temperature may seem strange, in the beginning. It is possible too, experience shows, for rise and fall to stop short at any point and mark a pause, more or less long, before resuming, or reversing, the rise now fall, the fall rise, these in their turn to be completed, or to stop short and mark a pause, more or less long, before resuming, or again reversing, and so on, till finally one or the other extreme is reached. Such variations of rise and fall, combining in countless rhythms, commonly attend the passage from white and heat to black and cold, and vice versa. The extremes alone are stable as is stressed by the vibration to be observed when a pause occurs at some intermediate stage, no matter what its level and duration. Then all vibrates, ground, wall, vault, bodies, ashen or leaden or between the two, as may be. But on the whole, experience shows, such uncertain passage is not common. And most often, when the light begins to fail, and along with it the heat, the movement continues unbroken until, in the space of some twenty seconds, pitch black is reached and at the same instant say freezing-point. Same remark for the reverse movement, towards heat and whiteness. Next most frequent is the fall or rise with pauses of varying length in these feverish greys, without at any moment reversal of the movement. But whatever its uncertainties the return sooner or later to a temporary calm seems assured, for the moment, in the black dark or the great whiteness, with attendant temperature, world still proof against enduring tumult. Rediscovered miraculously after what absence in perfect voids it is no longer quite the same, from this point of view, but there is no other. Externally all is as before and the sighting of the little fabric quite as much a matter of chance, its whiteness merging in the surrounding whiteness. But go in and now briefer lulls and never twice the same storm. Light and heat remain linked as though supplied by the same source of which still no trace. Still on the ground, bent in three, the head against the wall at B, the arse against the wall at A, the knees against the wall between B and C, the feet against the wall between C and A, that is to say inscribed in the semicircle ACB, merging in the white ground were it not for the long hair of strangely imperfect whiteness, the white body of a woman finally. Similarly inscribed in the other semicircle, against the wall his head at A, his arse at B, his knees between A and D, his feet between D and B, the partner. On their right sides therefore both and back to back head to arse. Hold a mirror to their lips, it mists. With their left hands they hold their left legs a little below the knee, with their right hands their left arms a little above the elbow. In this agitated light, its great white calm now so rare and brief, inspection is not easy. Sweat and mirror notwithstanding they might well pass for inanimate but for the left eyes which at incalculable intervals suddenly open wide and gaze in unblinking exposure long beyond what is humanly possible. Piercing pale blue the effect is striking, in the beginning. Never the two gazes together except once, when the beginning of one overlapped the end of the other, for about ten seconds. Neither fat nor thin, big nor small, the bodies seem whole and in fairly good condition, to judge by the surfaces exposed to view. The faces too, assuming the two sides of a piece, seem to want nothing essential. Between their absolute stillness and the convulsive light the contrast is striking, in the beginning, for one who still remembers having been struck by the contrary. It is clear however, from a thousand little signs too long to imagine, that they are not sleeping. Only murmur ah, no more, in this silence, and at the same instant for the eye of prey the infinitesimal shudder instantaneously suppressed. Leave them there, sweating and icy, there is better elsewhere. No, life ends and no, there is nothing elsewhere, and no question now of ever finding again that white speck lost in whiteness, to see if they still lie still in the stress of that storm, or of a worse storm, or in the black dark for good, or the great whiteness unchanging, and if not what they are doing.

Translated from the French by the author

PING

PING

All known all white bare white body fixed one yard legs joined like sewn. Light heat white floor one square yard never seen. White walls one yard by two white ceiling one square yard never seen. Bare white body fixed only the eyes only just. Traces blurs light grey almost white on white. Hands hanging palms front white feet heels together right angle. Light heat white planes shining white bare white body fixed ping fixed elsewhere. Traces blurs signs no meaning light grey almost white. Bare white body fixed white on white invisible. Only the eyes only just light blue almost white. Head haught eyes light blue almost white silence within. Brief murmurs only just almost never all known. Traces blurs signs no meaning light grey almost white. Legs joined like sewn heels together right angle. Traces alone unover given black light grey almost white on white. Light heat white walls shining white one yard by two. Bare white body fixed one yard ping fixed elsewhere. Traces blurs signs no meaning light grey almost white. White feet toes joined like sewn heels together right angle invisible. Eyes alone unover given blue light blue almost white. Murmur only just almost never one second perhaps not alone. Given rose only just bare white body fixed one yard white on white invisible. All white all known murmurs only just almost never always the same all known. Light heat hands hanging palms front white on white invisible. Bare white body fixed ping fixed elsewhere. Only the eyes only just light blue almost white fixed front. Ping murmur only just almost never one second perhaps a way out. Head haught eyes light blue almost white fixed front ping murmur ping silence. Eyes holes light blue almost white mouth white seam like sewn invisible. Ping murmur perhaps a nature one second almost never that much memory almost never. White walls each its trace grey blur signs no meaning light grey almost white. Light heat all known all white planes meeting invisible. Ping murmur only just almost never one second perhaps a meaning that much memory almost never. White feet toes joined like sewn heels together right angle ping elsewhere no sound. Hands hanging palms front legs joined like sewn. Head haught eyes holes light blue almost white fixed front silence within. Ping elsewhere always there but that known not. Eyes holes light blue alone unover given blue light blue almost white only colour fixed front. All white all known white planes shining white ping murmur only just almost never one second light time that much memory almost never. Bare white body fixed one yard ping fixed elsewhere white on white invisible heart breath no sound. Only the eyes given blue light blue almost white fixed front only colour alone unover. Planes meeting invisible one only shining white infinite but that known not. Nose ears white holes mouth white seam like sewn invisible. Ping murmurs only just almost never one second always the same all known. Given rose only just bare white body fixed one yard invisible all known without within. Ping perhaps a nature one second with image same time a little less blue and white in the wind. White ceiling shining white one square yard never seen ping perhaps way out there one second ping silence. Traces alone unover given black grey blurs signs no meaning light grey almost white always the same. Ping perhaps not alone one second with image always the same same time a little less that much memory almost never ping silence. Given rose only just nails fallen white over. Long hair fallen white invisible over. White scars invisible same white as flesh torn of old given rose only just. Ping image only just almost never one second light time blue and white in the wind. Head haught nose ears white holes mouth white seam like sewn invisible over. Only the eyes given blue fixed front light blue almost white only colour alone unover. Light heat white planes shining white one only shining white infinite but that known not. Ping a nature only just almost never one second with image same time a little less blue and white in the wind. Traces blurs light grey eyes holes light blue almost white fixed front ping a meaning only just almost never ping silence. Bare white one yard fixed ping fixed elsewhere no sound legs joined like sewn heels together right angle hands hanging palms front. Head haught eyes holes light blue almost white fixed front silence within. Ping elsewhere always there but that known not. Ping perhaps not alone one second with image same time a little less dim eye black and white half closed long lashes imploring that much memory almost never. Afar flash of time all white all over all of old ping flash white walls shining white no trace eyes holes light blue almost white last colour ping white over. Ping fixed last elsewhere legs joined like sewn heels together right angle hands hanging palms front head haught eyes white invisible fixed front over. Given rose only just one yard invisible bare white all known without within over. White ceiling never seen ping of old only just almost never one second light time white floor never seen ping of old perhaps there. Ping of old only just perhaps a meaning a nature one second almost never blue and white in the wind that much memory henceforth never. White planes no trace shining white one only shining white infinite but that known not. Light heat all known all white heart breath no sound. Head haught eyes white fixed front old ping last murmur one second perhaps not alone eye unlustrous black and white half closed long lashes imploring ping silence ping over.

Translated from the French by the author

LESSNESS

LESSNESS

Ruins true refuge long last towards which so many false time out of mind. All sides endlessness earth sky as one no sound no stir. Grey face two pale blue little body heart beating only upright. Blacked out fallen open four walls over backwards true refuge issueless.

Scattered ruins same grey as the sand ash grey true refuge. Four square all light sheer white blank planes all gone from mind. Never was but grey air timeless no sound figment the passing light. No sound no stir ash grey sky mirrored earth mirrored sky. Never but this changelessness dream the passing hour.

He will curse God again as in the blessed days face to the open sky the passing deluge. Little body grey face features crack and little holes two pale blue. Blank planes sheer white eye calm long last all gone from mind.

Figment light never was but grey air timeless no sound. Blank planes touch close sheer white all gone from mind. Little body ash grey locked rigid heart beating face to endlessness. On him will rain again as in the blessed days of blue the passing cloud. Four square true refuge long last four walls over backwards no sound.

Grey sky no cloud no sound no stir earth ash grey sand. Little body same grey as the earth sky ruins only upright. Ash grey all sides earth sky as one all sides endlessness.

He will stir in the sand there will be stir in the sky

the air the sand. Never but in dream the happy dream only one time to serve. Little body little block heart beating ash grey only upright. Earth sky as one all sides endlessness little body only upright. In the sand no hold one step more in the endlessness he will make it. No sound not a breath same grey all sides earth sky body ruins.

Slow black with ruin true refuge four walls over backwards no sound. Legs a single block arms fast to sides little body face to endlessness. Never but in vanished dream the passing hour long short. Only upright little body grey smooth no relief a few holes. One step in the ruins in the sand on his back in the endlessness he will make it. Never but dream the days and nights made of dreams of other nights better days. He will live again the space of a step it will be day and night again over him the endlessness.

In four split asunder over backwards true refuge issueless scattered ruins. Little body little block genitals overrun arse a single block grey crack overrun. True refuge long last issueless scattered down four walls over backwards no sound. All sides endlessness earth sky as one no stir not a breath. Blank planes sheer white calm eye light of reason all gone from mind. Scattered ruins ash grey all sides true refuge long last issueless.

Ash grey little body only upright heart beating face to endlessness. Old love new love as in the blessed days unhappiness will reign again. Earth sand same grey as the air sky ruins body fine ash grey sand. Light refuge sheer white blank planes all gone from mind. Flatness endless little body only upright same grey all sides earth sky body ruins. Face to white calm touch close eye calm long last all gone from mind. One step more one alone all alone in the sand no hold he will make it.

Blacked out fallen open true refuge issueless towards
which so many false time out of mind. Never but
silence such that in imagination this wild laughter
these cries. Head through calm eye all light white calm
all gone from mind. Figment dawn dispeller of
figments and the other called dusk.

He will go on his back face to the sky open again
over him the ruins the sand the endlessness. Grey air
timeless earth sky as one same grey as the ruins
flatness endless. It will be day and night again over
him the endlessness the air heart will beat again. True
refuge long last scattered ruins same grey as the sand.

Face to calm eye touch close all calm all white all
gone from mind. Never but imagined the blue in a wild
imagining the blue celeste of poesy. Little void mighty
light four square all white blank planes all gone from
mind. Never was but grey air timeless no stir not a
breath. Heart beating little body only upright grey
face features overrun two pale blue. Light white touch
close head through calm eye light of reason all gone
from mind.

Little body same grey as the earth sky ruins only
upright. No sound not a breath same grey all sides
earth sky body ruins. Blacked out fallen open four
walls over backwards true refuge issueless.

No sound no stir ash grey sky mirrored earth
mirrored sky. Grey air timeless earth sky as one same
grey as the ruins flatness endless. In the sand no hold
one step more in the endlessness he will make it. It will
be day and night again over him the endlessness the
air heart will beat again.

Figment light never was but grey air timeless no
sound. All sides endlessness earth sky as one no stir
not a breath. On him will rain again as in the blessed
days of blue the passing cloud. Grey sky no cloud no

sound no stir earth ash grey sand.

Little void mighty light four square all white blank planes all gone from mind. Flatness endless little body only upright same grey all sides earth sky body ruins. Scattered ruins same grey as the sand ash grey true refuge. Four square true refuge long last four walls over backwards no sound. Never but this changelessness dream the passing hour. Never was but grey air timeless no sound figment the passing light.

In four split asunder over backwards true refuge issueless scattered ruins. He will live again the space of a step it will be day and night again over him the endlessness. Face to white calm touch close eye calm long last all gone from mind. Grey face two pale blue little body heart beating only upright. He will go on his back face to the sky open again over him the ruins the sand the endlessness. Earth sand same grey as the air sky ruins body fine ash grey sand. Blank planes touch close sheer white all gone from mind.

Heart beating little body only upright grey face features overrun two pale blue. Only upright little body grey smooth no relief a few holes. Never but dream the days and nights made of dreams of other nights better days. He will stir in the sand there will be stir in the sky the air the sand. One step in the ruins in the sand on his back in the endlessness he will make it. Never but silence such that in imagination this wild laughter these cries.

True refuge long last scattered ruins same grey as the sand. Never was but grey air timeless no stir not a breath. Blank planes sheer white calm eye light of reason all gone from mind. Never but in vanished dream the passing hour long short. Four square all light sheer white blank planes all gone from mind.

Blacked out fallen open true refuge issueless towards

which so many false time out of mind. Head through calm eye all light white calm all gone from mind. Old love new love as in the blessed days unhappiness will reign again. Ash grey all sides earth sky as one all sides endlessness. Scattered ruins ash grey all sides true refuge long last issueless. Never but in dream the happy dream only one time to serve. Little body grey face features crack and little holes two pale blue.

Ruins true refuge long last towards which so many false time out of mind. Never but imagined the blue in a wild imagining the blue celeste of poesy. Light white touch close head through calm eye light of reason all gone from mind.

Slow black with ruin true refuge four walls over backwards no sound. Earth sky as one all sides endlessness little body only upright. One step more one alone all alone in the sand no hold he will make it. Ash grey little body only upright heart beating face to endlessness. Light refuge sheer white blank planes all gone from mind. All sides endlessness earth sky as one no sound no stir.

Legs a single block arms fast to sides little body face to endlessness. True refuge long last issueless scattered down four walls over backwards no sound. Blank planes sheer white eye calm long last all gone from mind. He will curse God again as in the blessed days face to the open sky the passing deluge. Face to calm eye touch close all calm all white all gone from mind.

Little body little block heart beating ash grey only upright. Little body ash grey locked rigid heart beating face to endlessness. Little body little block genitals overrun arse a single block grey crack overrun. Figment dawn dispeller of figments and the other called dusk.

THE LOST ONES

THE LOST ONES

Abode where lost bodies roam each searching for its lost one. Vast enough for search to be in vain. Narrow enough for flight to be in vain. Inside a flattened cylinder fifty metres round and sixteen high for the sake of harmony. The light. Its dimness. Its yellowness. Its omnipresence as though every separate square centimetre were agleam of the some twelve million of total surface. Its restlessness at long intervals suddenly stilled like panting at the last. Then all go dead still. It is perhaps the end of their abode. A few seconds and all begins again. Consequences of this light for the searching eye. Consequences for the eye which having ceased to search is fastened to the ground or raised to the distant ceiling where none can be. The temperature. It oscillates with more measured beat between hot and cold. It passes from one extreme to the other in about four seconds. It too has its moments of stillness more or less hot or cold. They coincide with those of the light. Then all go dead still. It is perhaps the end of all. A few seconds and all begins again. Consequences of this climate for the skin. It shrivels. The bodies brush together with a rustle of dry leaves. The mucous membrane itself is affected. A kiss makes an indescribable sound. Those with stomach still to copulate strive in vain. But they will not give in. Floor and wall are of solid rubber or suchlike. Dash against them foot or fist or head and the sound is scarcely heard. Imagine then the silence of the steps. The only sounds worthy of the name result from the manipulation of the ladders or the thud of bodies striking against one another or of one against itself as when in sudden fury it beats its breast. Thus flesh and bone subsist. The ladders. These are the only objects. They are single without exception and vary greatly in size. The shortest measure not less than six metres. Some are fitted with a sliding extension. They are propped against the wall without regard to harmony. Bolt upright on the top rung of the tallest the tallest climbers can touch the ceiling with their fingertips. Its composition is no less familiar therefore than that of floor and wall. Dash a rung against it and the sound is scarcely heard. These ladders are in great demand. At the foot of each at all times or nearly a little queue of climbers. And yet it takes courage to climb. For half the rungs are missing and this without regard to harmony. If only every second one were missing no great harm would be done. But the want of three in a row calls for acrobatics. These ladders are nevertheless in great demand and in no danger of being reduced to mere uprights runged at their extremities alone. For the need to climb is too widespread. To feel it no longer is a rare deliverance. The missing rungs are in the hands of a happy few who use them mainly for attack and self-defence. Their solitary attempts to brain themselves culminate at the best in brief losses of consciousness. The purpose of the ladders is to convey the searchers to the niches. Those whom these entice no longer climb simply to get clear of the ground. It is the custom not to climb two or more at a time. To the fugitive fortunate enough to find a ladder free it offers certain refuge until the clamours subside. The niches or alcoves. These are cavities sunk in that part of the wall which lies above an imaginary line running midway between floor and ceiling and features therefore of its upper half alone. A more or less wide mouth gives rapid access to a chamber of varying capacity but always sufficient for a body in reasonable command of its joints to enter in and similarly once in to crouch down after a fashion. They are disposed in irregular quincunxes roughly ten metres in diameter and cunningly out of line. Such harmony only he can relish whose long experience and detailed knowledge of the niches are such as to permit a perfect mental image of the entire system. But it is doubtful that such a one exists. For each climber has a fondness for certain niches and refrains as far as possible from the others. A certain number are connected by tunnels opened in the thickness of the wall and attaining in some cases no fewer than fifty metres in length. But most have no other way out than the way in. It is as though at a certain stage discouragement had prevailed. To be noted in support of this wild surmise the existence of a long tunnel abandoned blind. Woe the body that rashly enters here to be compelled finally after long efforts to crawl back backwards as best it can the way it came. Not that this drama is peculiar to the unfinished tunnel. One has only to consider what inevitably must ensue when two bodies enter a normal tunnel at the same time by opposite ends. Niches and tunnels are subject to the same light and climate as the rest of the abode. So much for a first aperçu of the abode.

One body per square metre or two hundred bodies in all round numbers. Whether relatives near and far or friends in varying degree many in theory are acquainted. The gloom and press make recognition difficult. Seen from a certain angle these bodies are of four kinds. Firstly those perpetually in motion. Secondly those who sometimes pause. Thirdly those who short of being driven off never stir from the coign they have won and when driven off pounce on the first free one that offers and freeze again. That is not quite accurate. For if among these sedentary the need to climb is dead it is none the less subject to strange resurrections. The quidam then quits his post in search of a free ladder or to join the nearest or shortest queue. The truth is that no searcher can readily forego the ladder. Paradoxically the sedentary are those whose acts of violence most disrupt the cylinder's quiet. Fourthly those who do not search or non-searchers sitting for the most part against the wall in the attitude which wrung from Dante one of his rare wan smiles. By non-searchers and despite the abyss to which this leads it is finally impossible to understand other than ex-searchers. To rid this notion of some of its virulence one has only to suppose the need to search no less resurrectable than that of the ladder and those eyes to all appearances for ever cast down or closed possessed of the strange power suddenly to kindle again before passing face and body. But enough will always subsist to spell for this little people the extinction soon or late of its last remaining fires. A languishing happily unperceived because of its slowness and the resurgences that make up for it in part and the inattention of those concerned dazed by the passion preying on them still or by the state of languor into which imperceptibly they are already fallen. And far from being able to imagine their last state when every body will be still and every eye vacant they will come to it unwitting and be so unawares. Then light and climate will be changed in a way impossible to foretell. But the former may be imagined extinguished as purposeless and the latter fixed not far from freezing point. In cold darkness motionless flesh. So much roughly speaking for these bodies seen from a certain angle and for this notion and its consequences if it is maintained.

Inside a cylinder fifty metres round and sixteen high for the sake of harmony or a total surface of roughly twelve hundred square metres of which eight hundred mural. Not counting the niches and tunnels. Omnipresence of a dim yellow light shaken by a vertiginous tremolo between contiguous extremes. Temperature agitated by a like oscillation but thirty or forty times slower in virtue of which it falls rapidly from a maximum of twenty-five degrees approximately to a minimum of approximately five whence a regular variation of five degrees per second. That is not quite accurate. For it is clear that at both extremes of the shuttle the difference can fall to as little as one degree only. But this remission never lasts more than a little less than a second. At great intervals suspension of the two vibrations fed no doubt from a single source and resumption together after a lull of varying duration but never exceeding ten seconds or thereabouts. Corresponding abeyance of all motion among the bodies in motion and heightened fixity of the motionless. Only objects fifteen single ladders propped against the wall at irregular intervals. In the upper half of the wall disposed quincuncially for the sake of harmony a score of niches some connected by tunnels.

From time immemorial rumour has it or better still the notion is abroad that there exists a way out. Those who no longer believe so are not immune from believing so again in accordance with the notion requiring as long as it holds that here all should die but with so gradual and to put it plainly so fluctuant a death as to escape the notice even of a visitor. Regarding the nature of this way out and its location two opinions divide without opposing all those still loyal to that old belief. One school swears by a secret passage branching from one of the tunnels and leading in the words of the poet to nature's sanctuaries. The other dreams of a trap-door hidden in the hub of the ceiling giving access to a flue at the end of which the sun and other stars would still be shining. Conversion is frequent either way and such a one who at a given moment would hear of nothing but the tunnel may well a moment later hear of nothing but the trapdoor and a moment later still give himself the lie again. The fact remains none the less that of these two persuasions the former is declining in favour of the latter but in a manner so desultory and slow and of course with so little effect on the comportment of either sect that to perceive it one must be in the secret of the gods. This shift has logic on its side. For those who believe in a way out possible of access as via a tunnel it would be and even without any thought of putting it to account may be tempted by its quest. Whereas the partisans of the trapdoor are spared this demon by the fact that the hub of the ceiling is out of reach. Thus by insensible degrees the way out transfers from the tunnel to the ceiling prior to never having been. So much for a first aperçu of this credence so singular in itself and by reason of the loyalty it inspires in the hearts of so many possessed. Its fatuous little light will be assuredly the last to leave them always assuming they are darkward bound.

Bolt upright on the top rung of the great ladder fully extended and reared against the wall the tallest climbers can touch the edge of the ceiling with their fingertips. On the same ladder planted perpendicular at the centre of the floor the same bodies would gain half a metre and so be enabled to explore at leisure the fabulous zone decreed out of reach and which therefore in theory is in no wise so. For such recourse to the ladder is conceivable. All that is needed is a score of determined volunteers joining forces to keep it upright with the help if necessary of other ladders acting as stays or struts. An instant of fraternity. But outside their explosions of violence this sentiment is as foreign to them as to butterflies. And this owing not so much to want of heart or intelligence as to the ideal preying on one and all. So much for this inviolable zenith where for amateurs of myth lies hidden a way out to earth and sky.

The use of the ladders is regulated by conventions of obscure origin which in their precision and the submission they exact from the climbers resemble laws. Certain infractions unleash against the culprit a collective fury surprising in creatures so peaceable on the whole and apart from the grand affair so careless of one another. Others on the contrary scarcely ruffle the general indifference. This at first sight is strange. All rests on the rule against mounting the ladder more than one at a time. It remains taboo therefore to the climber waiting at its foot until such time as his predecessor has regained the ground. Idle to imagine the confusion that would result from the absence of such a rule or from its non-observance. But devised for the convenience of all there is no question of its applying without restriction or as a licence for the unprincipled climber to engross the ladder beyond what is reasonable. For without some form of curb he might take the fancy to settle down permanently in one of the niches or tunnels leaving behind him a ladder out of service for good and all. And were others to

follow his example as inevitably they must the
spectacle would finally be offered of one hundred and
eighty-five searchers less the vanquished committed
for all time to the ground. Not to mention the
intolerable presence of properties serving no purpose.
It is therefore understood that after a certain interval
difficult to assess but unerringly timed by all the
ladder is again available meaning at the disposal in the
same conditions of him due next to climb easily
recognizable by his position at the head of the queue
and so much the worst for the abuser. The situation of
this latter having lost his ladder is delicate indeed and
seems to exclude a priori his ever returning to the
ground. Happily sooner or later he succeeds in doing
so thanks to a further provision giving priority at all
times to descent over ascent. He has therefore merely
to watch at the mouth of his niche for a ladder to
present itself and immediately start down quite easy in
his mind knowing full well that whoever below is on
the point of mounting if not already on his way up will
give way in his favour. The worst that can befall him is
a long vigil because of the ladders' mobility. It is
indeed rare for a climber when it comes to his turn to
content himself with the same niche as his predecessor
and this for obvious reasons that will appear in due
course. But rather he makes off with his ladder
followed by the queue and plants it under one or other
of the five niches available by reason of the difference
in number between these and the ladders. But to
return to the unfortunate having outstayed his time it
is clear that his chances of rapid redescent will be
increased though far from doubled if thanks to a
tunnel he disposes of two niches from which to watch.
Though even in this event he usually prefers and
invariably if the tunnel is a long one to plump for one

only lest a ladder should present itself at one or the other and he still crawling between the two. But the ladders do not serve only as vehicles to the niches and tunnels and those whom these have ceased if only temporarily to entice use them simply to get clear of the ground. They mount to the level of their choice and there stay and settle standing as a rule with their faces to the wall. This family of climbers too is liable to exceed the allotted time. It is in order then for him due next for the ladder to climb in the wake of the offender and by means of one or more thumps on the back bring him back to a sense of his surroundings. Upon which he unfailingly hastens to descend preceded by his successor who has then merely to take over the ladder subject to the usual conditions. This docility in the abuser shows clearly that the abuse is not deliberate but due to a temporary derangement of his inner timepiece easy to understand and therefore to forgive. Here is the reason why this in reality infrequent infringement whether on the part of those who push on up to the niches and tunnels or of those who halt on the way never gives rise to the fury vented on the wretch with no better sense than to climb before his time and yet whose precipitancy one would have thought quite as understandable and consequently forgivable as the converse excess. This is indeed strange. But what is at stake is the fundamental principle forbidding ascent more than one at a time the repeated violation of which would soon transform the abode into a pandemonium. Whereas the belated return to the ground hurts finally none but the laggard himself. So much for a first aperçu of the climbers' code.

Similarly the transport of the ladders is not left to the good pleasure of the carriers who are required to hug the wall at all times eddywise. This is a rule no less strict than the prohibition to climb more than one at a time and not lightly to be broken. Nothing more natural. For if for the sake of the shortcut it were permitted to carry the ladder slap through the press or skirting the wall at will in either direction life in the cylinder would soon become untenable. All along the wall therefore a belt about one metre wide is reserved for the carriers. To this zone those also are confined who wait their turn to climb and must close their ranks and flatten themselves as best they can with their backs to the wall so as not to encroach on the arena proper.

It is curious to note the presence within this belt of a certain number of sedentary searchers sitting or standing against the wall. Dead to the ladders to all intents and purposes and a source of annoyance for both climbers and carriers they are nevertheless tolerated. The fact is that these sort of semi-sages among whom all ages are to be admired from old age to infancy inspire in those still fitfully fevering if not a cult at least a certain deference. They cling to this as to a homage due to them and are morbidly susceptible to the least want of consideration. A sedentary searcher stepped on instead of over is capable of such an outburst of fury as to throw the entire cylinder into a ferment. Cleave also to the wall both sitting and standing four vanquished out of five. They may be walked on without their reacting.

To be noted finally the care taken by the searchers in the arena not to overflow on the climbers' territory. When weary of searching among the throng they turn towards this zone it is only to skirt with measured tread its imaginary edge devouring with their eyes its occupants. Their slow round counter-carrierwise creates a second even narrower belt respected in its turn by the main body of searchers. Which suitably lit from above would give the impression at times of two narrow rings turning in opposite directions about the teeming precinct.

One body per square metre of available surface or two hundred bodies in all round numbers. Bodies of either sex and all ages from old age to infancy. Sucklings who having no longer to suck huddle at gaze in the lap or sprawled on the ground in precocious postures. Others a little more advanced crawl searching among the legs. Picturesque detail a woman with white hair still young to judge by her thighs leaning against the wall with eyes closed in abandonment and mechanically clasping to her breast a mite who strains away in an effort to turn its head and look behind. But such tiny ones are comparatively few. None looks within himself where none can be. Eyes cast down or closed signify abandonment and are confined to the vanquished. These precisely to be counted on the fingers of one hand are not necessarily still. They may stray unseeing through the throng indistinguishable to the eye of flesh from the still unrelenting. These recognize them and make way. They may wait their turn at the foot of the ladders and when it comes ascend to the niches or simply leave the ground. They may crawl blindly in the tunnels in search of nothing. But normally abandonment freezes them both in space and in their pose whether standing or sitting as a rule profoundly bowed. It is this makes it possible to tell them from the sedentary devouring with their eyes in heads dead still each body as it passes by. Standing or sitting they cleave to the wall all but one in the arena stricken rigid in the midst of the fevering. These recognize him and keep their distance.

The spent eyes may have fits of the old craving just as those who having renounced the ladder suddenly take to it again. So true it is that when in the cylinder what little is possible is not so it is merely no longer so and in the least less the all of nothing if this notion is maintained. Then the eyes suddenly start to search afresh as famished as the unthinkable first day until for no clear reason they as suddenly close again or the head falls. Even so a great heap of sand sheltered from the wind lessened by three grains every second year and every following increased by two if this notion is maintained. If then the vanquished have still some way to go what can be said of the others and what better name be given them than the fair name of searchers? Some and indeed by far the greater number never pause except when they line up for a ladder or watch out at the mouth of a niche. Some come to rest from time to time all but the unceasing eyes. As for the sedentary if they never stir from the coign they have won it is because they have calculated their best chance is there and if they seldom or never ascend to the niches and tunnels it is because they have done so too often in vain or come there too often to grief. An intelligence would be tempted to see in these the next vanquished and continuing in its stride to require of those still perpetually in motion that they all soon or late one after another be as those who sometimes pause and of these that they finally be as the sedentary and of the sedentary that they be in the end as the vanquished and of the two hundred vanquished thus obtained that all in due course each in his turn be well and truly vanquished for good and all each frozen in his place and attitude. But let these families be numbered in order of maturity and experience shows that it is possible to graduate from one to three skipping two and from one to four skipping two or three or both and from two to four skipping three. In the other direction the ill-vanquished may at long intervals and with each relapse more briefly revert to the state of the sedentary who in their turn count a few chronic waverers prone to succumb to the ladder again while remaining dead to the arena. But never again will they ceaselessly come and go who now at long intervals come to rest without ceasing to search with their eyes. In the beginning then unthinkable as the end all roamed without respite including the nurselings in so far as they were borne except of course those already at the foot of the ladders or frozen in the tunnels the better to listen or crouching all eyes in the niches and so roamed a vast space of time impossible to measure until a first came to a standstill followed by a second and so on. But as to at this moment of time and there will be no other numbering the faithful who endlessly come and go impatient of the least repose and those who every now and then stand still and the sedentary and the so-called vanquished may it suffice to state that at this moment of time to the nearest body in spite of the press and gloom the first are twice as many as the second who are three times as many as the third who are four times as many as the fourth namely five vanquished in all. Relatives and friends are well represented not to speak of mere acquaintances. Press and gloom make recognition difficult. Man and wife are strangers two paces apart to mention only this most intimate of all bonds. Let them move on till they are close enough to touch and then without pausing on their way exchange a look. If they recognize each other it does not appear. Whatever it is they are searching for it is not that.

What first impresses in this gloom is the sensation of

yellow it imparts not to say of sulphur in view of the associations. Then how it throbs with constant unchanging beat and fast but not so fast that the pulse is no longer felt. And finally much later that ever and anon there comes a momentary lull. The effect of those brief and rare respites is unspeakably dramatic to put it mildly. Those who never know a moment's rest stand rooted to the spot often in extravagant postures and the stillness heightened tenfold of the sedentary and vanquished makes that which is normally theirs seem risible in comparison. The fists on their way to smite in anger or discouragement freeze in their arcs until the scare is past and the blow can be completed or volley of blows. Similarly without entering into tedious details those surprised in the act of climbing or carrying a ladder or making unmakable love or crouched in the niches or crawling in the tunnels as the case may be. But a brief ten seconds at most and the throbbing is resumed and all is as before. Those interrupted in their coming and going start coming and going again and the motionless relax. The lovers buckle to anew and the fists carry on where they left off. The murmur cut off as though by a switch fills the cylinder again. Among all the components the sum of which it is the ear finally distinguishes a faint stridulence as of insects which is that of the light itself and the one invariable. Between the extremes that delimit the vibration the difference is of two or three candles at the most. So that the sensation of yellow is faintly tinged with one of red. Light in a word that not only dims but blurs into the bargain. It might safely be maintained that the eye grows used to these conditions and in the end adapts to them were it not that just the contrary is to be observed in the slow deterioration of vision ruined by this fiery flickering murk and by the incessant straining for ever vain with concomitant moral distress and its repercussion on the organ. And were it possible to follow over a long enough period of time eyes blue for preference as being the most perishable they would be seen to redden more and more in an ever widening glare and their pupils little by little to dilate till the whole orb was devoured. And all by such slow and insensible degrees to be sure as to pass unperceived even by those most concerned if this notion is maintained. And the thinking being coldly intent on all these data and evidences could scarcely escape at the close of his analysis the mistaken conclusion that instead of speaking of the vanquished with the slight taint of pathos attaching to the term it would be more correct to speak of the blind and leave it at that. Once the first shocks of surprise are finally past this light is further unusual in that far from evincing one or more visible or hidden sources it appears to emanate from all sides and to permeate the entire space as though this were uniformly luminous down to its least particle of ambient air. To the point that the ladders themselves seem rather to shed than to receive light with this slight reserve that light is not the word. No other shadows then than those cast by the bodies pressing on one another wilfully or from necessity as when for example on a breast to prevent its being lit or on some private part the hand descends with vanished palm. Whereas the skin of a climber alone on his ladder or in the depths of a tunnel glistens all over with the same red-yellow glister and even some of its folds and recesses in so far as the air enters in. With regard to the temperature its oscillation is between much wider extremes and at a much lower frequency since it takes not less than four seconds to pass from its minimum of five degrees to its maximum of twenty-five and inversely namely an average of only five degrees per second. Does this mean that with every passing second there is a rise or fall of five degrees exactly neither more nor less? Not quite. For it is clear there are two periods in the scale namely from twenty-one degrees on on the way up and from nine on on the way down when this difference will not be reached. Out of the eight seconds therefore required for a single rise and fall it is only during a bare six and a half that the bodies suffer the maximum increment of heat or cold which with the help of a little addition or better still division works out nevertheless at some twenty years respite per century in this domain. There is something disturbing at first sight in the relative slowness of this vibration compared to that of the light. But this is a disturbance analysis makes short work of. For on due reflection the difference to be considered is not one of speed but of space travelled. And if that required of the temperature were reduced to the equivalent of a few candles there would be nothing to choose mutatis mutandis between the two effects. But that would not answer the needs of the cylinder. So all is for the best. The more so as the two storms have this in common that when one is cut off as though by magic then in the same breath the other also as though again the two were connected somewhere to a single commutator. For in the cylinder alone are certitudes to be found and without nothing but mystery. At vast intervals then the bodies enjoy ten seconds at most of unbroken warmth or cold or between the two. But this cannot be truly accounted for respite so great is the other tension then.

The bed of the cylinder comprises three distinct zones separated by clear-cut mental or imaginary frontiers invisible to the eye of flesh. First an outer belt roughly one metre wide reserved for the climbers and strange to say favoured by most of the sedentary and vanquished. Next a slightly narrower inner belt where those weary of searching in mid-cylinder slowly revolve in Indian file intent on the periphery. Finally the arena proper representing an area of one hundred and fifty square metres round numbers and chosen hunting ground of the majority. Let numbers be assigned to these three zones and it appears clearly that from the third to the second and inversely the searcher moves at will whereas on entering and leaving the first he is held to a certain discipline. One example among a thousand of the harmony that reigns in the cylinder between order and licence. Thus access to the climbers' reserve is authorized only when one of them leaves it to rejoin the searchers of the arena or exceptionally those of the intermediate zone. While infringement of this rule is rare it does none the less occur as when for example a particularly nervous searcher can no longer resist the lure of the niches and tries to steal in among the climbers without the warrant of a departure. Whereupon he is unfailingly ejected by the queue nearest to the point of trespass and the matter goes no further. No choice then for the searcher wishing to join the climbers but to watch for his opportunity among the searchers of the intermediate zone or searcher-watchers or simply watchers. So much for access to the ladders. In the other direction the passage is not free either and once among the climbers the watcher is there for some time and more precisely the highly variable time it takes to advance from the tail to the head of the queue adopted. For no less than the freedom for each body to climb is the obligation once in the queue of its choice to queue on to the end. Any attempt to leave prematurely is sharply countered by the other members and the offender put back in his place. But once at the very foot of the ladder with between him and it only one more return to the ground the aspirant is free to rejoin the searchers of the arena or exceptionally the watchers of the intermediate zone without opposition. It is therefore on those at the head of their lines as being the most likely to create the vacancy so ardently desired that the eyes of the second-zone watchers are fixed as they burn to enter the first. The objects of this scrutiny continue so up to the moment they exercise their right to the ladder and take it over. For the climber may reach the head of the queue with the firm resolve to ascend and then feel this melt little by little and gather in its stead the urge to depart but still without the power to decide him till the very last moment when his predecessor is actually on the way down and the ladder virtually his at last. To be noted also the possibility for the climber to leave the queue once he has reached the head and yet not leave the zone. This merely requires his joining one of the other fourteen queues at his disposal or more simply still his returning to the tail of his own. But it is exceptional for a body in the first place to leave its queue and in the second having exceptionally done so not to leave the zone. No alternative then once among the climbers but to stay there at least the time it takes to advance from the last place to the first of the chosen queue. This time varies according to the length of the latter and the more or less prolonged occupation of the ladder. Some users keep it till the last moment. For others one half or any other fraction of this time is enough. The short queue is not necessarily the most rapid and such a one starting tenth may well find himself first before such another starting fifth assuming of course they start together. This being so no wonder that the choice of the queue is determined by considerations having nothing to do with its length. Not that all choose nor even the greater number. The tendency would be rather to join straightway the queue nearest to the point of penetration on condition however that this does not involve motion against the stream. For one entering this zone head-on the nearest queue is on the right and if it does not please it is only by going right that a more pleasing can be found. Some could thus revolve through thousands of degrees before settling down to wait were it not for the rule forbidding them to exceed a single circuit. Any attempt to elude it is quelled by the queue nearest to the point of full circle and the culprit compelled to join its ranks since obviously the right to turn back is denied him too. That a full round should be authorized is eloquent of the tolerant spirit which in the cylinder tempers discipline. But whether chosen or first to hand the queue must be suffered to the end before the climber may leave the zone. First chance of departure therefore at any moment between arrival at head of queue and predecessor's return to ground. There remains to clarify in this same context the situation of the body which having accomplished its queue and let pass the first chance of departure and exercised its right to the ladder returns to the ground. It is now free again to depart without further ado but with no compulsion to do so. And to remain among the climbers it has merely to join again in the same conditions as before the queue so lately left with departure again possible from the moment the head is reached. And should it for some reason or another feel like a little change of queue and ladder it is entitled for the purpose of fixing its choice to a further full circuit in the same way as on first arrival and in the same conditions with this slight difference that having already suffered one queue to the end it is free at any moment of the new revolution to leave the zone. And so on infinitely. Whence theoretically the possibility for those already among the climbers never to leave and never to arrive for those not yet. That there exists no regulation tending to forestall such injustice shows clearly it can never be more than temporary. As indeed it cannot. For the passion to search is such that no place may be left unsearched. To the watcher nevertheless on the qui vive for a departure the wait may seem interminable. Sometimes unable to endure it any longer and fortified by the long vacation he renounces the ladder and resumes his search in the arena. So much roughly speaking for the main ground divisions and the duties and prerogatives of the bodies in their passage from one to another. All has not been told and never shall be. What principle of priority obtains among the watchers always in force and eager to profit by the first departure from among the climbers and whose order of arrival on the scene cannot be established by the queue impracticable in their case or by any other means? Is there not reason to fear a saturation of the intermediate zone and what would be its consequences for the bodies as a whole and particularly for those of the arena thus cut off from the ladders? Is not the cylinder doomed in a more or less distant future to a state of anarchy given over to fury and violence? To these questions and many more the answers are clear and easy to give. It only remains to dare. The sedentary call for no special remark since only the ladders can wean them from their fixity. The vanquished are obviously in no way concerned.

The effect of this climate on the soul is not to be

underestimated. But it suffers certainly less than the skin whose entire defensive system from sweat to goose bumps is under constant stress. It continues none the less feebly to resist and indeed honourably compared to the eye which with the best will in the world it is difficult not to consign at the close of all its efforts to nothing short of blindness. For skin in its own way as it is not to mention its humours and lids it has not merely one adversary to contend with. This desiccation of the envelope robs nudity of much of its charm as pink turns grey and transforms into a rustling of nettles the natural succulence of flesh against flesh. The mucous membrane itself is affected which would not greatly matter were it not for its hampering effect on the work of love. But even from this point of view no great harm is done so rare is erection in the cylinder. It does occur none the less followed by more or less happy penetration in the nearest tube. Even man and wife may sometimes be seen in virtue of the law of probabilities to come together again in this way without their knowledge. The spectacle then is one to be remembered of frenzies prolonged in pain and hopelessness long beyond what even the most gifted lovers can achieve in camera. For male or female all are acutely aware how rare the occasion is and how unlikely to recur. But here too the desisting and deathly still in attitudes verging at times on the obscene whenever the vibrations cease and for as long as this crisis lasts. Stranger still at such times all the questing eyes that suddenly go still and fix their stare on the void or on some old abomination as for instance other eyes and then the long looks exchanged by those fain to look away. Irregular intervals of such length separate these lulls that for forgetters the likes of these each is the first. Whence invariably the same vivacity of reaction as to the end of a world and the same brief amaze when the twofold storm resumes and they start to search again neither glad nor even sorry.

Seen from below the wall presents an unbroken surface all the way round and up to the ceiling. And yet its upper half is riddled with niches. This paradox is explained by the levelling effect of the dim omnipresent light. None has even been known to seek out a niche from below. The eyes are seldom raised and when they are it is to the ceiling. Floor and ceiling bear no sign or mark apt to serve as a guide. The feet of the ladders pitched always at the same points leave no trace. The same is true of the skulls and fists dashed against the wall. Even did such marks exist the light would prevent their being seen. The climber making off with his ladder to plant it elsewhere relies largely on feel. He is seldom out by more than a few centimetres and never by more than a metre at most because of the way the niches are disposed. On the spur of his passion his agility is such that even this deviation does not prevent him from gaining the nearest if not the desired niche and thence though with greater labour from regaining the ladder for the descent. There does none the less exist a north in the guise of one of the vanquished or better one of the women vanquished or better still the woman vanquished. She squats against the wall with her head between her knees and her legs in her arms. The left hand clasps the right shinbone and the right the left forearm. The red hair tarnished by the light hangs to the ground. It hides the face and whole front of the body down to the crutch. The left foot is crossed on the right. She is the north. She rather than some other among the vanquished because of her greater fixity. To one bent for once on taking his bearings she may be of help. For the climber averse to avoidable acrobatics a given niche may lie so many paces or metres to east or west of the woman vanquished without of course his naming her thus or otherwise even in his thoughts. It goes without saying that only the vanquished hide their faces though not all without exception. Standing or sitting with head erect some content themselves with opening their eyes no more. It is of course forbidden to withhold the face or other part from the searcher who demands it and may without fear of resistance remove the hand from the flesh it hides or raise the lid to examine the eye. Some searchers there are who join the climbers with no thought of climbing and simply in order to inspect at close hand one or more among the vanquished or sedentary. The hair of the woman vanquished has thus many a time been gathered up and drawn back and the head raised and the face laid bare and whole front of the body down to the crutch. The inspection once completed it is usual to put everything carefully back in place as far as possible. It is enjoined by a certain ethics not to do unto others what coming from them might give offence. This precept is largely observed in the cylinder in so far as it does not jeopardize the quest which would clearly be a mockery if in case of doubt it were not possible to check certain details. Direct action with a view to their elucidation is generally reserved for the persons of the sedentary and vanquished. Face or back to the wall these normally offer but a single aspect and so may have to be turned the other way. But wherever there is motion as in the arena or among the watchers and the possibility of encompassing the object there is no call for such manipulations. There are times of course when a body has to be brought to a stand and disposed in a certain position to permit the inspection at close hand of a particular part or the search for a scar or birthblot for example. To be noted finally the immunity in this respect of those queueing for a ladder. Obliged for want of space to huddle together over long periods they appear to the observer a mere jumble of mingled flesh. Woe the rash searcher who carried away by his passion dare lay a finger on the least among them. Like a single body the whole queue falls on the offender. Of all the scenes of violence the cylinder has to offer none approaches this.

So on infinitely until towards the unthinkable end if this notion is maintained a last body of all by feeble fits and starts is searching still. There is nothing at first sight to distinguish him from the others dead still where they stand or sit in abandonment beyond recall. Lying down is unheard of in the cylinder and this pose solace of the vanquished is for ever denied them here. Such privation is partly to be explained by the dearth of floor space namely a little under one square metre at the disposal of each body and not to be eked out by that of the niches and tunnels reserved for the search alone. Thus the prostration of those withered ones filled with the horror of contact and compelled to brush together without ceasing is denied its natural end. But the persistence of the twofold vibration suggests that in this old abode all is not yet quite for the best. And sure enough there he stirs this last of all if a man and slowly draws himself up and some time later opens his burnt eyes. At the foot of the ladders propped against the wall with scant regard to harmony no climber waits his turn. The aged vanquished of the third zone has none about him now but others in his image motionless and bowed. The mite still in the white-haired woman's clasp is no more than a shadow in her lap. Seen from the front the red head sunk to the uttermost exposes part of the nape. There he opens then his eyes this last of all if a man and some time later threads his way to that first among the vanquished so often taken for a guide. On his knees he parts the heavy hair and raises the unresisting head. Once devoured the face thus laid bare the eyes at a touch of the thumbs open without demur. In those calm wastes he lets his wander till they are the first to close and the head relinquished falls back into its place. He himself after a pause impossible to time finds at last his place and pose whereupon dark descends and at the same instant the temperature comes to rest not far from freezing point. Hushed in the same breath the faint stridulence mentioned above whence suddenly such silence as to drown all the faint breathings put together. So much roughly speaking for the last state of the cylinder and of this little people of searchers one first of whom if a man in some unthinkable past for the first time bowed his head if this notion is maintained.